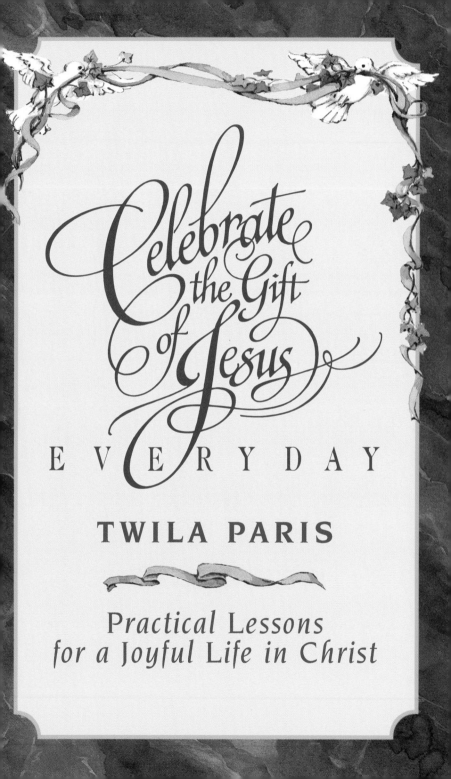

Celebrate the Gift of Jesus

EVERYDAY

TWILA PARIS

Practical Lessons
for a Joyful Life in Christ

Celebrate the Gift of Jesus

E V E R Y D A Y

Twila Paris

Practical Lessons
for a Joyful Life in Christ

Artwork by Victoria Marshall

WARNER
Press

Designed by Roger Hoffman, Dianne Deckert
Edited by Tammy Tilley

Scriptures taken from the HOLY BIBLE: NEW INTERNATIONAL VERSION.
Copyright © 1973, 1978, 1984 by the International Bible Society.
Used by permission of Zondervan Bible Publishers.

Devotional text copyright © 1993 by Twila Paris.
Art, graphics, and design copyright ©1994 by Warner Press, Inc.
ALL RIGHTS RESERVED.

ISBN: 0-87162-667-5   Stock #: D7550
Printed in Mexico
Warner Press, Inc.

CELEBRATE THE GIFT
Words by Twila Paris, Dwight Liles, Darrell Harris & Allen Koppelberger; Music by Ken Abraham & Tink
Abraham. ©Copyright 1993 Ariose Music/ASCAP, Shepherd's Fold Music/BMI (divisions of Star Song
Communications) & Mountain Spring Music/ASCAP. Administrated by Gaither Copyright Management.
All rights reserved. Used by permission.

HE IS EXALTED
Words and music by Twila Paris. ©Copyright 1985 by StraightWay Music (a division of Star Song
Communications) & Mountain Spring Music. All rights reserved.
Used by permission of Gaither Copyright Management.

KEEPIN' MY EYES ON YOU
Words and music by Twila Paris. ©Copyright 1982 Singspiration Music/ASCAP. All Rights Reserved.
Used by permission of Benson Music Group, Inc.

RUNNER
Written by Twila and Starla Paris. ©Copyright 1985 by StraightWay Music (a division of Star Song
Communications) & Mountain Spring Music. All rights reserved.
Used by permission of Gaither Copyright Management.

BONDED TOGETHER
Words and music by Twila Paris. ©Copyright 1987 by Ariose Music (a division of Star Song Communications)
& Mountain Spring Music. All rights reserved. Used by permission of Gaither Copyright Management.

HOW BEAUTIFUL
Words and music by Twila Paris. ©Copyright 1990 by Ariose Music (a division of Star Song Communications)
& Mountain Spring Music. All rights reserved. Used by permission of Gaither Copyright Management.

WE WILL GLORIFY
Words and music by Twila Paris. ©Copyright 1982 Singspiration Music/ASCAP. All Rights Reserved.
Used by permission of Benson Music Group, Inc.

EVERY HEART THAT IS BREAKING
Words and music by Twila Paris. ©Copyright 1988 by Ariose Music (a division of Star Song Communications)
& Mountain Spring Music. All rights reserved. Used by permission of Gaither Copyright Management.

DESTINY
Words and music by Twila Paris. ©Copyright 1992 by Ariose Music (a division of Star Song Communications)
& Mountain Spring Music. All rights reserved. Used by permission of Gaither Copyright Management.

This book is dedicated to my family
whose lives and words have inspired
so much of what I have to share.

TABLE OF CONTENTS

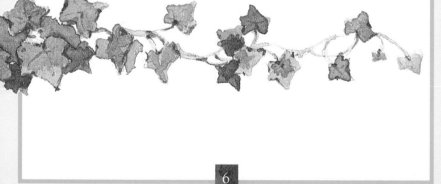

TO THE READER:

Jesus: a precious Gift given to us from God. God chose to offer His Son to us not only so we would have eternal life with Him, but also to teach us about living joyfully in *this* life. *Celebrate the Gift of Jesus Every Day: Practical Lessons for a Joyful Life in Christ* helps us discover and celebrate the beauty, freedom, and joy in living for Christ. Like His direction, the lessons are clear; like Jesus' truths, the words are simple. Whether we seek guidance on loving others, on beginning our day with praise, or on overcoming heartache and disillusionment, God provides a plan for us. This book helps to highlight some of His wise words.

Each lesson has been written in such a way that no matter where you are on your spiritual journey, you will discover basic truths, encouraging words, and challenging insights to help lead you forward. Each thought, coupled with scriptures and a brief prayer, can be meditated on, applied, and lifted up to God as you strive to live joyfully in His plan.

Celebrate the Gift of Jesus Every Day has been prayed over by all involved in its composition. More than anything else, the purpose of this book is to speak to your heart, to challenge you, and to move you toward a life of complete celebration and dependence on our Sovereign God … not only in sporadic moments, but every day. God bless you as you read and discover again the joy of living in the love of Christ.

CELEBRATE
THE GIFT

Pure and perfect are His gifts
Coming down from above;
Chosen with care, bought with a price,
Wrapped in our Father's love.
Let His people rejoice
With one heart, with one voice....

Come as you are to the Holy Child,
Son of God, Lord Most High.
Open your heart, you will receive
A gift you cannot buy.
Here is hope, ever new;
Let it be born in you.

Celebrate the gift of Jesus;
Celebrate the King.
Celebrate the gift of Jesus—
The reason that we sing.
O come, let us adore Him,
Lift our hearts in praise.
Celebrate the love of the Father;
Celebrate the gift of Jesus.

Everyday Moments *with the* *Father*

He is exalted,
the King is exalted on high;
I will praise Him.
He is exalted, forever exalted,
and I will praise His name.
He is the Lord; forever His truth shall reign.
Heaven and earth rejoice in His holy name:
He is exalted, the King is exalted on high.

(HE IS EXALTED)

May the words of my mouth
and the meditation of my heart
be pleasing in your sight, O Lord,
my Rock and my Redeemer.
PSALM 19:14

*W*e have a wonderful opportunity to commit

our words and thoughts to the Lord each morning,

before we go out to face the challenges and

adventures of the day! Whether in the car, in the

kitchen, or just in the quietness of our hearts,

we can pray, "Let the words of my mouth and the

meditation of my heart be pleasing to You,

O Lord." Our Lord is always pleased when His

children long to be in His presence.

P r a y e r :
May all that I do, say, and feel today be pleasing
to You, Lord, the Giver and Maker of all good things.

Within your temple, O God,
we meditate on your unfailing love.
PSALM 48:9

Love the Lord your God
with all your heart and with all your soul
and with all your mind....
Love your neighbor as yourself.

MATTHEW 22:37, 39

What matters most to God is that we love

Him passionately, with all that is within us. Every

action should be motivated by our love for God;

every word should be an outpouring of it.

Loving God is our highest priority. It is also

our greatest privilege.

P r a y e r :
Above all else, Father, today I choose to love You
and to love others. Thank You for being
the ultimate example of love.

Know this love that surpasses knowledge—
that you may be filled to the measure
of all the fullness of God.

EPHESIANS 3:19

Through Jesus, therefore,
let us continually offer to God
a sacrifice of praise—
the fruit of lips that confess his name.

HEBREWS 13:15

When we daily offer ourselves as living

sacrifices to God, our lives are filled with wonderful

fruit for our benefit as well as for the Kingdom

of God. We give ourselves to God not because we

feel noble for doing so, but simply because it

is appropriate. All praise goes to God our Father,

the source and the continuance of all good things.

P r a y e r :
Jesus, even when I may not feel joyful, I can still offer
a sacrifice of praise to You. I trust that, in time, You will
restore that wonderful joy that comes whenever I simply
voice my thanks to You, my Sovereign God.

Give thanks to the Lord, for he is good....
To him who alone does great wonders, ...
who by his understanding
made the heavens,
His love endures forever.

PSALM 136:1, 4, 5

Those who know your name will trust in you,
for you, Lord, have never forsaken those who seek you.
PSALM 9:10

 $\mathcal{W}$ e trust in God because of His faithfulness.

The more we know of the Father, the easier it is

to trust Him. We discovered God's faithfulness

in yesterday's trials, and we know that God's Word

will still hold true tomorrow. God does not forsake

those who seek Him.

P r a y e r :
Lord, You promise that when I seek You, I will *always* find
You. Today I cling to that simple but awesome promise!

God, who has called you into fellowship
with his Son Jesus Christ our Lord, is faithful.
1 CORINTHIANS 1:9

When I consider your heavens, the work of your fingers,
the moon and the stars, which you have set in place,
what is man that you are mindful of him,
the son of man that you care for him?

PSALM 8:3, 4

We can easily forget where we came from
and where we would be without God. Sometimes
we even forget that God is sovereign! When our
hearts are in the right place, we will be filled
with wonder that the Creator of the universe
has chosen to lift us up … to care for us …
and to receive us to Him.

Prayer:
Whenever I think that You, the Creator of the world,
also chose and purposed my life, I feel humbled,
I am honored, and I give thanks.

All … comes from the Lord Almighty,
wonderful in counsel and magnificent in wisdom.

ISAIAH 28:29

He is the faithful God, keeping his covenant of love
to a thousand generations of those
who love him and keep his commands.

DEUTERONOMY 7:9

When we know someone well, and we love
and trust this person implicitly, we assume the
best about him or her, even if circumstances
indicate otherwise. God wants to be that kind
of friend to us, but it will happen only when we
choose to spend time alone with Him. If we know
God intimately, our faith in Him will never
be based on our circumstances, but *always*
on His unchanging character.

P r a y e r :
How reassuring it is to know, Lord, that although
the ebb and flow of life changes, You *never* change.
Your constancy is a blessing to my heart.

Let us hold unswervingly to the hope we profess,
for he who promised is faithful.

HEBREWS 10:23

*T*oday I remind myself once again that God

owes me nothing, but has given me everything

in His Son. It is my incredible privilege simply

to be called to worship the most high God ...

in love, in humility, and in reverence.

P r a y e r :
Without Your sovereign love and will, Lord,
I would not exist. Today I simply give thanks that You
love me enough to give me life and a brand new day
to spend time with You.

As for God, his way is perfect;
the word of the Lord is flawless.
He is a shield for all who take refuge in him.
PSALM 18:30

Be sure to fear the Lord and serve him faithfully
with all your heart;
consider what great things he has done for you.
1 SAMUEL 12:24

When the things we say and think are
pleasing to God, then the things we do will also
reflect God's pleasure. If we daily seek God's face
and meditate upon His promises, love, and
character, our actions will follow—all because
we take the time to seek the Father.

P r a y e r :
May I be reminded to seek Your face
on this day, Lord; may my actions reflect Christ …
and may You be pleased.

Look to the Lord and his strength;
seek his face always.
PSALM 105:4

GOD'S PRINCIPLES:

Everyday Gifts to Live By

Lord, I'm keeping my eyes on You,
Following You, following You, my Lord—
I'm keeping my eyes on You....
I won't look to the left or right;
My only goal is keeping You in my sight;
Lord, I'm keeping my eyes on You.

(KEEPIN' MY EYES ON YOU)

You are my portion, O Lord;
I have promised to obey your words.
I have sought your face with all my heart;
be gracious to me according to your promise.

PSALM 119:57, 58

*L*ong ago the Judge of the earth gave us laws and principles by which to govern our lives. Throughout the ages, humankind has proved repeatedly that obedience to God's principles brings life and disobedience brings death. Whenever God's children continually and willingly choose to disobey His laws, they find themselves walking in a dry, parched land. But when they instead choose to obey God and follow Him, they eventually discover sweet victory when they are led to the fountain of Living Water!

P r a y e r :
Today, Lord, I choose to live joyfully by Your law ...
and I know that I will discover a deeper, richer life
than I have ever imagined or experienced before.

Whoever believes in me ...
streams of living water will flow from within him.

JOHN 7:38

The law from your mouth is more precious to me
than thousands of pieces of silver and gold.

PSALM 119:72

*G*od's principles are precious treasures that

He has given us. If we seek first after gold and

earthly treasures and fail to hold dear God's truth,

we will be continually frustrated, discontented,

and brokenhearted. But if we will obey God's laws,

listen to His words, heed His warnings, and follow

His guidelines, God's laws will always be a source

of great joy in our lives … and we will be

truly fulfilled.

P r a y e r :
You gave me rules to live by, not to punish me, Lord,
but to steer me from danger. May I live by Your Word
so that I can know the pure joy that comes
from living for You.

Blessed are they who keep his statutes
and seek him with all their heart.

PSALM 119:2

I know that the Lord saves his anointed....
Some trust in chariots and some in horses,
but we trust in the name of the Lord our God.

PSALM 20:6, 7

Whenever we put our faith in human

inventions and earthly powers to help us through

the day, we will always live to regret it. But those

who trust in the name of the Lord have no regret.

God responds to our trust with faithfulness;

His faithfulness is our reward.

P r a y e r :
You have blessed me with the mental capacity to think
through problems I face in a given day; but remind me,
Lord, that nothing is a substitute for praying and looking
to You, the Author of my faith.

Let us fix our eyes on Jesus,
the author and perfecter of our faith.

HEBREWS 12:2

The law of the Lord is perfect, reviving the soul.
The statutes of the Lord are trustworthy.
PSALM 19:7

*S*ome people say that God's laws are not valid and His principles no longer apply in this enlightened society. Believing that the rules have been changed and the boundaries moved, millions of blinded souls step over the lines every day because it feels good or seems right. In reality, the lines of good and evil have never moved an inch since they were drawn by the hand of God. But God *will* move all of heaven and earth to bring one lost soul back into the fold … and He has.

P r a y e r :
What comfort and security I find in knowing
that You, God, are the same forever.
Your truth is as constant as Your love.

Jesus Christ is the same
yesterday and today and forever.
HEBREWS 13:8

If my people, who are called by my name,
will humble themselves and pray and seek my face ...
then will I hear from heaven ...
and will heal their land.

2 CHRONICLES 7:14

*P*ride is often the greatest source of all
that is bad in our lives. Pride results in separation
from others, from God's perfect plan for our lives,
and worst of all from God Himself. The proud
person will ultimately fail. But when we look
to God and humbly give our lives to the Lord,
we will inevitably succeed in becoming mature
children of God—simply because God has
promised to make sure we do.

P r a y e r :
I look to You today, Lord, as the true example of humility,
and I willingly choose to put my pride aside,
regardless of the circumstance ... and follow You.

[God] gives grace to the humble....
Humble yourselves before the Lord,
and he will lift you up.

JAMES 4:6, 10

God is my salvation; I will trust and not be afraid.
The Lord ... is my strength and my song;
he has become my salvation.

ISAIAH 12:2

*G*od gives us tools to work with—

systems, partners, helpers, and financial provision.

Sometimes transferring faith from God to tangible

and visible resources is easy to do. But only God

is capable of being our salvation. Only God

is always faithful. Only God can be trusted

with our lives.

P r a y e r :
Thank You for meeting my needs ...
and for reminding me that You, not things,
are the source of my happiness and salvation.

This is the Lord, we trusted in him;
let us rejoice and be glad in his salvation.

ISAIAH 25:9

Come, let us go up to the mountain of the Lord....
He will teach us his ways,
so that we may walk in his paths.
MICAH 4:2

*A*s children of God, we have an awesome

responsibility to hold up the truth for others

to see. At the same time, we must keep our own

eyes fixed on Jesus so that we will be protected

from the subtle deception of this Age. When our

hearts and minds are focused on Christ, our lives

will reflect Christ's love.

P r a y e r :
When I give You my heart, Lord, You protect it. May I
show the world the victory and confidence that comes
only from knowing that You take care of me
whenever I look to You.

The peace of God, which transcends all understanding,
will guard your hearts and your minds in Christ Jesus.
PHILIPPIANS 4:7

As iron sharpens iron,
so one man sharpens another.
PROVERBS 27:17

*O*ne of the most challenging ways we learn to live by God's principles is through other believers. We can be grateful for brothers and sisters in Christ who care enough about us to tell us of an area of weakness in our lives that they have observed. Their words may be difficult for us to hear at first, but in the end, truth ministers life to us. We are blessed to have friends who live by God's principles and who share His principles with us, even when sharing means taking a risk.

P r a y e r :
Thank You, God, for friends who love me even in the tough times when it is difficult to love. I find great comfort in knowing that they are committed not only to our friendship, but to truth, and to You.

Faithful are the wounds
of a friend.
PROVERBS 27:6

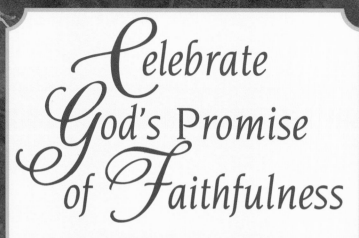

Celebrate God's Promise of Faithfulness

Obstacle ancient, chilling the way;
Enemy wakened, stoking the fray.
Still be determined, fearless and true,
Lift high the standard; carry it through....

Mindful of many waiting to run,
Destined to finish what you've begun;
Millions before you cheering you on,
Godspeed, dear runner, carry it home....

Runner, when the road is long,
Feel like giving in, but you're hanging on—
Oh, runner, when the race is won,
You will run into His arms.

(RUNNER)

*He said to me, "My grace is sufficient for you,
for my power is made perfect in weakness."*

2 CORINTHIANS 12:9

*G*od's children experience a wonderful

sense of security in knowing that the grace of God

is always available and sufficient. No matter what

the situation or how difficult the circumstance,

if we only accept God's grace, we will be able

to function in the strength of God rather than

in our own weakness.

P r a y e r :
Because You know the struggles in my life, God,
empower me with Your strength and grace
so that together, we can conquer anything.

*In your hands are strength and power
to exalt and give strength to all.*

1 CHRONICLES 29:12

I press on toward the goal to win the prize
for which God has called me heavenward
in Christ Jesus.
PHILIPPIANS 3:14

A successful person is *not* one who has never failed, but rather one who, when he does fail, will try again. There is not a single Christian who has never made a mistake. But the worst mistake is to allow failure—or even the fear of failure— to paralyze us. Perseverance and persistance are true signs of courage and strength even when we make mistakes; and the greatest source of this strength is Jesus Christ.

P r a y e r :
Help me remember that You, my Saviour, do not
expect perfection from me; You only request that I
press on toward the goal.

Let us throw off everything that hinders
and the sin that so easily entangles,
and let us run with perseverance
the race marked out for us.
HEBREWS 12:1

Do not worry about your life, what you will eat;
or about your body, what you will wear....
Your Father knows that you need them.
But seek his kingdom,
and these things will be given to you as well.

LUKE 12:22, 30, 31

*I*f we become too anxious about our earthly provision and the future, perhaps we're not trusting God's promises. When we give our cares to the Lord, we discover the good life that comes from trusting in the Father: peace, joy, and contentment ... for today, tomorrow, and forever.

P r a y e r :
I know Your strong but gentle hand will guide me through all my tomorrows, dear Father, because it is the same faithful hand that has helped me in the past.

Because you are my help,
I sing in the shadow of your wings.
I stay close to you;
your right hand upholds me.

PSALM 63:7, 8

How great is your goodness,
which you have stored up
for those who fear you,
which you bestow in the sight of men
on those who take refuge in you.

PSALM 31:19

*S*ometimes we think that if certain problems would go away, then we would be able to give thanks to God and no longer be hindered by such trials. When the situation is resolved, we move on without giving thought or thanks to God for His sustaining power. On the other hand, if we just pause and recognize God's grace in the midst of turmoil, we just might discover that our problem isn't so insurmountable after all.

P r a y e r :
Help me to thank You even in the tough times, God—
maybe not *for* them, but because You are faithful
to be with me *throughout* them.

The Lord gives strength to his people;
the Lord blesses his people with peace.

PSALM 29:11

You will keep in perfect peace
him whose mind is steadfast,
because he trusts in you.
ISAIAH 26:3

*W*orries about this life can serve as a spiritual
barometer to believers, indicating if their priorities
are aligned to the will of God. Jesus promises a
peace that passes understanding. This peace will
keep us from the anxieties that would rob us
of the wonderful relationship that God wants us
to have with Him. God's peace, or the world's
worry: it's our choice.

P r a y e r :
Peace is Your promised gift. I find it when I give all my
burdens to You, my personal Prince of Peace.

Peace I leave with you; my peace I give you.
I do not give to you as the world gives.
Do not let your hearts be troubled
and do not be afraid.
JOHN 14:27

There are different kinds of gifts,
but the same Spirit.... Now to each one
the manifestation of the Spirit
is given for the common good.

1 CORINTHIANS 12:4, 7

 We experience an incredible freedom when we realize that everything we have and everything we are comes from God. Our abilities and talents are given by our Father, and He is the one who brings these gifts to their full potential. God lovingly gives us special abilities, and when we use them for His glory, we discover the pure joy and freedom that only comes from living our lives for Christ.

P r a y e r :

God, one of the great paradoxes of life is when I give
my all to You, in return I find the kind of freedom that I
would not have found in any other way. You make my life
so much richer, so much more meaningful,
and I give You thanks.

Fan into flame the gift of God,
which is in you.

2 TIMOTHY 1:6

f you're walking forward but fall flat on your face, at least you fall forward; so just by getting up and stepping out again, you have gained a little ground. There is spiritual truth in this physical application. The victorious Christian is the one who, when he falls, gets back up on his feet, forgets what is behind … and presses on.

P r a y e r :
Forgive my preoccupation with failure, Father.
Instead, help me to focus on You, for if I do fall,
I know that Your loving arms will catch me.

"Not by might nor by power,
but by my Spirit,"
says the Lord Almighty.
ZECHARIAH 4:6

*O*ur problems change when our focus changes. When we focus on our problems, we discover heartache, disillusionment, and despair. When we focus on God, even in the midst of our pain, we discover peace, stability, and strength. God wants to give us a fresh perspective.

P r a y e r :
Teach me to focus on You and not on my problems, Lord, to depend on Your strength and not on my own "wisdom." Together, I know we can make it.

I can do everything through him
who gives me strength.
PHILIPPIANS 4:13

Celebrate the Family of God

Like a tightly woven garment, like a metal alloy,
We are put together in the strongest way.
With a common bond to join us
that they cannot destroy,
We are held together in the longest way;
And we could not be pulled apart
Without it tearing out a heart.

Bonded together,
You are my Father forever;
You will never leave me.
We are bonded together.

(BONDED TOGETHER)

I will be a Father to you,
and you will be my sons and daughters,
says the Lord Almighty.

2 CORINTHIANS 6:18

*N*othing seems sweeter and more secure than the picture of a father holding his child's hand as they walk together. God wants to be just like that father to you by providing security, support, and companionship. Your heavenly Father's firm, yet loving hand will gently take hold of your hand and help keep you steady. You are God's child, and you are loved.

P r a y e r :
You, O God, spoke the universe into order, and You love me enough to call me Your child. What a wonderful privilege I have to call You Father!

You did not receive a spirit
that makes you a slave again to fear,
but you received the Spirit of sonship.
And by him we cry, "Abba, Father."

ROMANS 8:15

To all who received him,
to those who believed in his name,
he gave the right to become children of God.

JOHN 1:12

*S*ome people inherit a wonderful spiritual

heritage for which they can be very thankful;

others, unfortunately, may not have grown up

in a home where God was revered. What comfort

and reassurance we have when we become

Christians! The family of God becomes our family,

and God is our Father. All things become new,

and our heritage as a child of God is the most

beautiful of all.

P r a y e r :
Thank You that regardless of my earthly circumstances,
You are still my eternal Father ... and forever Friend.

You are no longer foreigners and aliens,
but fellow citizens with God's people
and members of God's household.

EPHESIANS 2:19

You anoint my head with oil; my cup overflows.
Surely goodness and love will follow me
all the days of my life,
and I will dwell in the house of the Lord forever.

PSALM 23:5, 6

*G*od has such a tender heart toward each
of His children. He truly cares about the stresses
and painful circumstances in our lives. No matter
how busy we are, we must give our Father the time
to lead us beside still waters and anoint our heads
with oil—because only God can truly restore a
tired and hurting soul.

P r a y e r :
Whenever I am frightened or insecure, I am comforted
by Your promise to hold my hand, Lord. Whenever
my faith is shaken, I am comforted by
Your promise to hold my heart.

The Father of compassion
and the God of all comfort …
comforts us in all our troubles.

2 CORINTHIANS 1:3, 4

You will call, and the Lord will answer;
you will cry for help, and he will say:
Here am I.
ISAIAH 58:9

*P*icture yourself actually living with God

in the same house ... talking with Him during the

day, listening to His wise counsel. As God speaks

with you, He ministers comfort, encouragement,

and correction, even in your sleep. If you are

always aware of the very real and close presence

of God, you will not be swayed by the pressures

of life. Give thanks, and give praise ... for your

heavenly Father walks with you on this day.

P r a y e r :
It is so easy to let the world take my attention away
from You, my heavenly Father. Please direct my eyes
to Your loving smile; please direct my ears
to Your loving voice.

Your ears will hear a voice behind you, saying,
"This is the way; walk in it."
ISAIAH 30:21

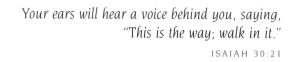

45

The Lord is my strength and my shield;
my heart trusts in him, and I am helped....
The Lord is the strength of his people,
a fortress of salvation for his anointed one.

PSALM 28:7, 8

*W*hether we are baby Christians or have been

given some degree of leadership responsibility,

we must all remember that God is our source

of strength, comfort, and protection. We never

outgrow the need to run home to the Father

when we've been overwhelmed by our battles.

If we will honestly pour out our hurts and fears

to Him, our loving Father will graciously bind up

our wounds and equip us for future victories.

God loves the child inside the armor.

P r a y e r :
Thank You for the promise that whenever I run to You,
I will find You waiting ... with Your arms open and
outstretched, ready to hold me.

He heals the brokenhearted
and binds up their wounds.

PSALM 147:3

Do not lose heart when he rebukes you,
because the Lord disciplines those he loves.
HEBREWS 12:5, 6

*W*henever we receive correction from God,

our human impulse is to struggle and resist similar

to the small child who runs in circles to avoid

discipline. But like the caring, nurturing parent,

God's correction proves once more His great love

for us. God cares enough to discipline us and help

conform us to the image of His Son ... and that

is one of the most loving things our heavenly

Father can do for us.

P r a y e r :
Even as an adult, I sometimes find difficulty in receiving
correction, God. But You teach me that if I am open
to Your discipline, I will discover the peace You offer.
Thank You for teaching me the difference between
being childish and child-like.

Lead me, O Lord,
in your righteousness ...
make straight your way before me.
PSALM 5:8

In love he predestined us to be adopted
as his sons through Jesus Christ,
in accordance with his pleasure and will.
EPHESIANS 1:4, 5

*W*hen we become Christians, old things pass away. If we did not grow up in a Christian family, we can choose to become a part of Christ's family and pass down a godly heritage to our children, and to our children's children. They will be blessed because of our faithfulness, and we will be abundantly blessed that our families will inherit the Kingdom along with us.

P r a y e r :
What an incredible reminder, Lord, that when I choose to follow You, future generations may be affected by my choice. Today, I choose You as Father, and I rejoice in knowing that those who follow might choose You as well.

Your Father has been pleased
to give you the kingdom.
LUKE 12:32

Search me, O God, and know my heart;
test me and know my anxious thoughts.
See if there is any offensive way in me,
and lead me in the way everlasting.

PSALM 139:23, 24

*G*od is the *only* one who knows each of us better than we know ourselves. We are sometimes wrong about the condition of our own hearts; we tend to be too hard on ourselves in some areas and too easy in others. But when we ask the Father to search our hearts, His truth goes directly to the core like a laser. If we allow it, God will lovingly and gently remove all that should not be there, and replace it with what should be.

P r a y e r :

Forgive me whenever I wrongfully believe that I know myself better than You know me, Lord. You spoke my life into existence; surely I can trust that You know my heart.

I will praise the Lord, who counsels me;
even at night my heart instructs me.
I have set the Lord always before me....
I will not be shaken.

PSALM 16:7, 8

49

Sharing the Gift of Jesus

How beautiful the heart that bled,
That took all my sin and bore it instead.
How beautiful the tender eyes
That choose to forgive and never despise.
How beautiful, how beautiful,
How beautiful is the body of Christ....

How beautiful the feet that bring
The sound of good news and the love of the King.
How beautiful the hands that serve
The wine and the bread and the sons of the earth.
How beautiful, how beautiful,
How beautiful is the body of Christ.

(HOW BEAUTIFUL)

Let your conversation be always full of grace,
seasoned with salt, so that you may know
how to answer everyone.

COLOSSIANS 4:6

*M*any Christian brothers and sisters who
regularly speak openly about their faith share one
thing in common: they radiate the love and
graciousness of Christ in their words. Gracious
speech without compromise is what attracts
people, believers and unbelievers, to God's
everlasting message. Christ's words establish the
example of communicating grace. The Holy Spirit
can empower us with the same kind of speech so
that others will be passionately drawn to the truth
and love of Christ.

P r a y e r :
Father, empower me today to speak with passion and
grace about Your love. May my words bring another lamb
into Your fold.

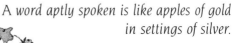

A word aptly spoken is like apples of gold
in settings of silver.

PROVERBS 25:11

Teach us to number our days aright,
that we may gain a heart of wisdom....
Establish the work of our hands for us—
yes, establish the work of our hands.
PSALM 90:12, 17

$\mathcal{W}$e will not live forever; with God's help we

can set our priorities accordingly. We can pray that

the work of our hands will be established by God

so that we will accomplish the things that really

matter for the Kingdom of God—not just for now

in the eyes of people, but ten thousand years from

now in the eyes of God.

P r a y e r :
May all that I do and say today fulfill a single purpose—
to glorify Your name and Your Kingdom forever!

There is a time for everything,
and a season for every activity under heaven....
He has made everything beautiful in its time.
He has also set eternity in the hearts of men.
ECCLESIASTES 3:1, 11

In your teaching show integrity,
seriousness and soundness of speech
that cannot be condemned.
TITUS 2:7, 8

ometimes in our humanness we fall prey

to spreading a bad report about someone,

perhaps because we suddenly feel more holy

by comparison or even vindicated in our own

weakness. The Spirit of God can guard our tongues

and prompt our spirits at these moments

of temptation. With God's help we can speak words

that uplift another person and edify our Lord.

God will be honored ... and we will be blessed.

P r a y e r :
Forgive me, Lord, when I say anything that does not
reflect Your compassion and love. Help me speak words
that will honor You and encourage or help my Christian
brothers and sisters.

Pleasant words are a honeycomb,
sweet to the soul
and healing to the bones.
PROVERBS 16:24

The word of the Lord came to me, saying,
"Before I formed you in the womb I knew you,
before you were born I set you apart....
I have put my words in your mouth."

JEREMIAH 1:4, 5, 9

*G*od has set us apart and given us the

privilege to carry the eternal good news to those

who desperately need hope for a brighter

tomorrow. We need not be afraid to speak.

We need not feel too inadequate or inarticulate.

God says, "I have put my words in your mouth."

We can say and do things that far exceed our own

abilities when God empowers us to speak His

truth. His Spirit will give us the words;

we need only to trust that He will.

P r a y e r :
I believe You when You say that You will give me
the words to speak Your truth; help me, O God,
to believe in myself. Together, we can share
Your wonderful news of love!

The Lord said ...
"I will help you speak
and will teach you what to say."

EXODUS 4:11, 12

What does the Lord your God ask of you
but to fear the Lord your God,
to walk in all his ways, to love him,
to serve the Lord your God
with all your heart and with all your soul?

DEUTERONOMY 10:12

*T*rue ministry is always an extension of true relationship with God. If we get so busy telling others how to have a relationship with God but we neglect our own time with Him, our words will eventually become empty and shallow. But if we will first look to God and then take His love to the world, God will be pleased. And lives—including our own—will be changed.

P r a y e r :
Sometimes I try to minister to others through my own power and abilities instead of through Christ. Remind me, Lord, that when I look to You first and then share Your love with others, people will see Christ like never before.

Serve wholeheartedly, as if you
were serving the Lord, not men.

EPHESIANS 6:7

Do not be afraid; keep on speaking,
do not be silent. For I am with you.
ACTS 18:9, 10

*G*od is sending a new generation out in His

name and authority to speak His words to the

nations, and each of us must answer this question:

Will I be obedient to God's call in my life?

P r a y e r :
You ask me to speak Your truth and love to a hurting
world. I answer a resounding YES to Your call.
May You find me faithful today.

Go ... and tell the people
the full message of this new life.
ACTS 5:20

Well done, good and faithful servant!
You have been faithful with a few things;
I will put you in charge of many things.
Come and share your master's happiness!
MATTHEW 25:23

$\mathcal{S}$ometimes we grow frustrated

or discontented because God isn't using us

in the time or way we believe is best. But God

doesn't demand that we take giant steps in our

ministry or take on monumental tasks in our

service to Him; God asks that we be faithful

in our current place of responsibility. Our

faithfulness to God will provide us with more

opportunities to minister to others than we ever

would have dreamed.

P r a y e r :

Lord, Your own ministry focused on teaching the twelve
disciples, and then empowering them to share Your love
with others. May I not try to change an entire
neighborhood or community instantaneously.
Help me simply love one person at a time.

If anyone serves,
he should do it with the strength God provides,
so that in all things
God may be praised through Jesus Christ.
I PETER 4:11

Be very careful, then, how you live—
not as unwise but as wise,
making the most of every opportunity.

EPHESIANS 5:15, 16

A familiar adage proclaims:

Only one life will soon be past;

Only what's done for Christ will last.

Life on earth is not eternal, but our actions and

words do have eternal consequences. The most

important thing to achieve in a day is to give and

serve in the name of the Lord. Whether a kind word

is gently spoken or a good deed is gladly

performed, we can know the pure joy that comes

simply from living one day, one moment, at a time,

in the goodness and grace of the Lord.

P r a y e r :
Days quickly pass, and seasons come and go,
but my prayer each morning remains the same:
Lord, through my life this day, may You be glorified.

May the glory of the Lord endure forever;
may the Lord rejoice in his works.

PSALM 104:31

Our Gift to God:

Living for Jesus

We will glorify the King of kings,
We will glorify the Lamb.
We will glorify the Lord of lords;
Who is the great I Am....

He is Lord of heaven, Lord of earth,
He is Lord of all who live.
He is Lord above the universe;
All praise to Him we give.

(WE WILL GLORIFY)

My command is this:
Love each other as I have loved you.
JOHN 15:12

*L*ove is commonly thought of as an emotion, and in some cases, an uncontrollable one. By commanding us to love one another, God tells us that He considers love to be a choice. God also makes it clear that true love is very practical in nature: Love is expressed in how we use our hands, our time, even our finances. We love others with more than our hearts; we love others with all our ability. Love is always about what we do, and ultimately about who we are.

P r a y e r :
Dear Lord, today I choose to love, even if at times I don't
"feel" love. In my words and actions, may I be a reflection
of You and Your everlasting love.

*Dear friends, let us love one another,
for love comes from God.
Everyone who loves has been born of God
and knows God.*
1 JOHN 4:7

62

Be kind and compassionate to one another,
forgiving each other,
just as in Christ God forgave you.
EPHESIANS 4:32

When we were children, we learned about being kind, tenderhearted, and forgiving to others. These ideas seemed so simple to grasp at the time. As adults, these same ideas can seem elusive, maybe because we have experienced pain or unfulfilled dreams and expectations. But God does not give us permission to leave these truths behind as we move on in our faith. God promises that when we show these qualities to the world, we show the world the character of God.

Prayer:

I pray for revival, God, for rededication to You and Your example of kindness, forgiveness, and love. May that revival begin in my own heart.

As God's chosen people, holy and dearly loved,
clothe yourselves with compassion, kindness,
humility, gentleness and patience.
Bear with each other and forgive whatever grievances
you may have against one another.
COLOSSIANS 3:12, 13

If you spend yourselves in behalf of the hungry
and satisfy the needs of the oppressed,
then your light will rise in the darkness,
and your night will become like the noonday.

ISAIAH 58:10

enerosity in the name of the Lord to those in need is a very wise investment. God promises that when we are in trouble, the Lord will deliver us, and we will be blessed by Him. Likewise, when our brothers or sisters are in trouble, we can follow Christ's example by giving of ourselves. Whether we give in money or time, we show the world God's gift of mercy.

P r a y e r :
God, I am humbled by Your generosity—that You gave Your Son to die for me. Today may You be pleased that I willingly give myself back to You.

Freely you have received, freely give.

MATTHEW 10:8

We pray … that you may live a life worthy
of the Lord and may please him in every way:
bearing fruit in every good work,
growing in the knowledge of God.

COLOSSIANS 1:10

*F*ruit is a natural by-product of a tree or vine

that is genuine, healthy, and planted in the right

soil. The presence or absence of these qualities

in our lives demonstrates whether or not we

are truly living and walking in the Spirit of God.

By knowing and understanding the fruit of the

Spirit as well as their bounty, we can hold them up

as character goals. But more importantly, we must

focus on an intimate relationship with Christ.

When we truly belong to God and are full

of the Spirit, the fruit will grow naturally …

and will be genuine.

P r a y e r :
Thank You for reminding me of the simple truth, Lord,
that my relationship with You will not grow until I do my
part to nurture it. Today may You find me firmly planted
in Your love and growing in Your Word.

The fruit of the Spirit is love, joy, peace, patience,
kindness, goodness, faithfulness, gentleness and self-control.
Against such things there is no law.

GALATIANS 5:22, 23

65

Sing joyfully to the Lord, you righteous;
it is fitting for the upright to praise him.

PSALM 33:1

*T*he Bible says that praise is becoming to the upright, so we are set apart from the rest of the world simply in the act of worship and praise to God. Whenever we speak or sing words of joy and praise to our heavenly Father, our faces will radiate to the world our love for God. And if praise is this beautiful on the outside to the human eye, how much more beautiful it must be on the inside, to the eyes of our loving God.

P r a y e r :
Today I ask for nothing, Father. I simply offer my praise to You. Blessing and honor be unto Your holy name!

You are a chosen people, a royal priesthood …
a people belonging to God,
that you may declare the praises of him
who called you out of darkness
into his wonderful light.

1 PETER 2:9

Serve the Lord with gladness;
come before him with joyful songs....
Enter his gates with thanksgiving
and his courts with praise; give thanks to him
and praise his name.

PSALM 100:2, 4

*G*ratefulness is the opposite of self-pity.

We discover little time and energy in our lives

for self-pity when we instead choose to meditate

on the mercy and goodness of God. Thankfulness

flows from our hearts and mouths when we spend

our time praising God for His blessings and

faithfulness to us. As we grow in becoming

consistently joyful and enthusiastic servants,

we also bring joy to the heart of our Lord.

P r a y e r :

Grant me a spirit of gratefulness, Lord. Fill me with Your
mercy so I can praise You with all my heart and soul. You,
O God, are deserving of my thanks both today and forever.

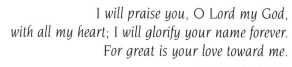

I will praise you, O Lord my God,
with all my heart; I will glorify your name forever.
For great is your love toward me.

PSALM 86:12, 13

May the Lord make your love increase
and overflow for each other and for everyone else.

1 THESSALONIANS 3:12

*L*ove cannot be love if it is self-contained. Love must be freely given and expressed. The evidence and definition of God's love is not only found in what we say or even in what we feel, but in how we show love to another. When we look to Christ as our example of love, we discover a love that is shared with another, whether in word or in deed. Christ's love is all-encompassing.

P r a y e r :
Lord, You have shown that love is not without cost—
in time, energy, or even comfort. But You have also shown
that love is worth the risk. Make me more willing to risk,
more able to love.

Live a life of love, just as Christ loved us
and gave himself up for us
as a fragrant offering
and sacrifice to God.

EPHESIANS 5:2

The Lord your God ... is gracious and compassionate,
slow to anger and abounding in love.
JOEL 2:13

*C*hrist is our perfect example of kindness, tenderness, and forgiveness. He changed water into wine at a wedding, even though the time was not ideal for Him to display His power. Christ lovingly washed the feet of His disciples the night before He died. And when Christ hung from the cruel cross, He spoke a prayer of forgiveness for those who crucified Him. God asks that we follow Christ's perfect example by being kind to a sometimes cruel world, tenderhearted to those who may misunderstand us, and forgiving to those who hurt us. The task may be difficult at times, but our loving Saviour truly understands and will always give us the ability to live for Him.

P r a y e r :

You accept me fully and forgive me completely, Lord. Your mercies are never-ending. I praise You for being the perfect example of love.

When you stand praying, if you hold
anything against anyone, forgive him,
so that your Father in heaven may forgive you.
MARK 11:25

Jesus: The One Who Came to Heal

For the young abandoned husband
Left alone without a reason,
For the pilgrim in the city where there is no home …
For the son without a father,
For his solitary mother,
I have a message:
He sees you, He knows you, He loves you….

For the precious, fallen daughter,
For her devastated father,
For the prodigal who's dying in a strange new way …
For the child who's always hungry,
For the patriot with no country,
I have a message:
He sees you, He knows you, He loves you….

Every heart that is breaking tonight
Is the heart of a child
That He holds in His sight
And, oh, how He longs to hold in His arms
Every heart that is breaking tonight.

(EVERY HEART THAT IS BREAKING)

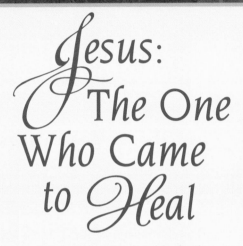

He got up and rebuked the wind
and the raging waters; the storm subsided,
and all was calm.

LUKE 8:24

*S*ome of the most frightening storms can
be inside your own heart. God's voice can calm
the storm of turmoil and fear just as surely as His
voice stilled the winds and the water. Take a
moment apart from the assault of the day, and
come into your rest. Jesus is with you.

P r a y e r :
When the darkness of my days leaves me frightened,
I am comforted when You guide me. When the storms
threaten my faith, I am comforted when You protect me.
Thank You, Father of Comfort.

Come to me,
all you who are weary and burdened,
and I will give you rest....
For I am gentle and humble in heart,
and you will find rest for your souls.

MATTHEW 11:28, 29

Do not fear, for I am with you;
do not be dismayed, for I am your God.
I will strengthen you and help you;
I will uphold you with my righteous right hand.

ISAIAH 41:10

*I*n spite of our careful maneuvering, we inevitably come face-to-face with pain. We confront stressful circumstances we can't control or even understand. Yet in the midst of our unanswered questions, we can feel God's presence. He walks through the pain with us, offering His hand of strength. We may not understand why we must suffer, but accepting God's comfort and love during the pain provides us with the strength to endure.

P r a y e r :
I may not understand why Your children should
sometimes experience pain, Lord, but I pray for
greater trust that You will be with me during
stressful times, ministering words of comfort and love.
You care both about my character and my heart.

The Lord is close to the brokenhearted
and saves those who are crushed in spirit.

PSALM 34:18

Encourage one another
and build each other up,
just as in fact you are doing.
1 THESSALONIANS 5:11

*S*ome people have healing personalities: just being with them makes a hurting person feel better. Usually people who are good at comforting others have also suffered, and therefore understand other people's pain. But these people probably chose out of brokenness to reach to our heavenly Father and allow God to bring comfort and peace. If we are hurting today, we can also go to God for comfort. If we are willing, He will turn our sorrow into a healing balm that we can, in turn, pour out on those around us.

P r a y e r :
Thank You for all those times when I heard Your loving voice in the words of a friend. May I also be Your hand of comfort to another who is hurting today.

The God of all grace,
who called you to his eternal glory in Christ,
after you have suffered a little while, will himself restore you
and make you strong, firm and steadfast.
1 PETER 5:10

*The angel of the Lord
encamps around those who fear him,
and he delivers them.*

PSALM 34:7

*O*ften the most committed Christians suffer

the greatest attacks because they are on the front

lines. Battles are fought in the spiritual realm, and

the wounds hurt just as deeply as physical wounds.

Yet even in the midst of the battle, we can trust

that the spiritual battle has already been fought

and the final victory has already been won. God

and His children remain the winners for eternity.

P r a y e r :
You are bigger than any question, stronger than any foe,
O Lord. I am comforted by knowing that and strengthened
by believing it. When I encounter spiritual conflicts,
I feel secure in knowing that You have already
helped me to win the battle.

*The weapons we fight with
are not the weapons of the world.
On the contrary, they have divine power
to demolish strongholds.*

2 CORINTHIANS 10:4

I know what it is to be in need,
and I know what it is to have plenty.
I have learned the secret
of being content in any and every situation.

PHILIPPIANS 4:12

*P*robably very few of us reach the point where
we are able to honestly say, "I take pleasure in
infirmities and persecutions," but we can rejoice
in knowing that Christ can receive glory from them.
Christ's strength is made perfect in our weakness.
We can show the world that when Christians suffer,
God heals our hurts.

P r a y e r :
Your Word reminds me that I will experience trials. During
these times, help me not to rely on my own strength, for
then I will fail. Help me to rely on You, the greatest source
of strength and comfort I will find.

In me you may have peace.
In this world you will have trouble.
But take heart!
I have overcome the world.

JOHN 16:33

The Lord is near. Do not be anxious about anything,
but in everything,... present your requests to God.
And the peace of God, which transcends all understanding,
will guard your hearts and your minds in Christ Jesus.

PHILIPPIANS 4:5-7

On the outside, our lives can appear orderly

and together. We can seem completely calm so

that even our best friends don't realize when we're

filled with raging anxieties, fears, or dread. But

Christ knows exactly how we feel and why we feel

the way we do. Because Christ already knows our

hearts—and fears—we don't need to pretend with

Him. He is waiting for us to ask Him to comfort us

in our fears ... and He will.

P r a y e r :
All-knowing God, I can keep no secrets from You. You
know my every thought, each hope and dream, my worries
and concerns. I lay them all before You, trusting You'll
take care of them—and me.

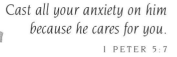

Cast all your anxiety on him
because he cares for you.

I PETER 5:7

We also rejoice in our sufferings,
because we know that suffering produces perseverance;
perseverance, character; and character, hope.
And hope does not disappoint us, because God has
poured out his love into our hearts by the Holy Spirit.
ROMANS 5:3-5

*W*e often see God working in other people's lives through their suffering, but we cannot help but hope that our lives will be exempt from pain. We hope that we can learn the things we need to learn just by hearing and reading about them. But like our fellow believers who have also suffered, we ultimately recognize that the greatest gifts and the deepest foundations have been results of circumstances we never would have chosen.

P r a y e r :
Life is not a reflection of You, God. Life is not always fair
or kind. But You are *always* these things and so much
more. You are never-changing. You are always beside me.
I thank You with all my heart.

Do not let your hearts be troubled.
Trust in God; trust also in me....
I will not leave you as orphans;
I will come to you.
JOHN 14:1, 18

Our struggle is not against flesh and blood,
but ... against the powers of this dark world....
Therefore put on the full armor of God,
so that when the day of evil comes,
you may be able to stand your ground.
EPHESIANS 6:12, 13

*I*n our turbulent moments when battles

rage, God brings comfort to our troubled hearts,

and His Holy Spirit infuses us with power to

withstand the onslaught of the enemy. We can

decide daily to stand, pick up the weapons God

has given us, and put on the belt of truth and

shield of faith. Truly God has equipped and

prepared us for battle. We can be ready

by wearing the armor.

P r a y e r :
Thank You, Father, for loving me enough
to equip me for the battles I must endure ...
and for standing and fighting with me throughout them.

Let us ... put on
the armor of light.
ROMANS 13:12

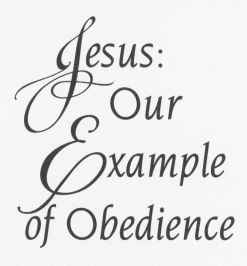

Jesus: Our Example of Obedience

Do you know Him?
This is your destiny;
When you obey Him,
There is an open door.
Do you believe …
And will you love Him?
This is your destiny.
When you obey Him,
There is an open door
To your unspoken dream.

(DESTINY)

Jesus … made himself nothing,
taking the very nature of a servant, …
humbled himself and became obedient to death—
even death on a cross!
Therefore God exalted him.

PHILIPPIANS 2:5, 7-9

*J*esus Christ came into this world and left with no honors: born in a lowly stable, buried in a borrowed tomb. His only desire was to do the will of the Father. That should be our main desire, too.

P r a y e r :

Jesus, You designed salvation for the world by choosing to suffer and die. You chose to express Your love in the greatest possible way. Today, I choose to love You back. I choose to serve You. I choose to be obedient to Your call.

Humble yourselves before the Lord,
and he will lift you up.

JAMES 4:10

Whatever you do, work at it with all your heart,
as working for the Lord, not for men,
since you know that you will receive
an inheritance from the Lord.

COLOSSIANS 3:23, 24

If we as Christians would always keep

in mind for whom we are really working, then

we would consistently stand out as the most

productive and efficient segment of society. Paul

challenges us to work with all our hearts, whatever

our task: doing homework, cooking dinner, building

cars, or performing surgery. Whenever we perform

our duties as to the Lord, our work becomes a

practical way of being obedient to God, as well as

showing Him praise and honor.

P r a y e r :
Whatever my vocation or status in life, my ultimate goal is
to please You, Lord. May my every word and deed
be toward that goal.

I will obey your word.
Open my eyes that I may see
wonderful things in your law.
PSALM 119:17, 18

You yourselves are our letter, written on our hearts …
not with ink but with the Spirit of the living God,
not on tablets of stone but on tablets of human hearts.
2 CORINTHIANS 3:2, 3

*W*e do not live in a spiritual vacuum. Our actions have far-reaching and eternal consequences in our own lives and in the lives of those close to us. But we also affect the lives of more people than we can imagine, many more than we know or see personally in a day. God's model for us is interdependence, as Jesus exemplified in His friendships with the disciples. Although we are not responsible for the actions of others, we are responsible for the results of our own actions upon other people's lives. By living in interdependence, we support, depend upon, and guide each other … just as God intended.

P r a y e r :

God, I realize that sometimes my actions speak louder than my words. I pray that my actions will reflect the words I say so that those who may be watching me will receive a glimpse of You.

Look not only to your own interests,
but also to the interests of others.
PHILIPPIANS 2:4

Does the Lord delight in burnt offerings and sacrifices
as much as in obeying the voice of the Lord?
To obey is better than sacrifice.

1 SAMUEL 15:22

*W*hen we were children and we feared being

reprimanded for our disobedience, we may have

attempted to influence our parents' discipline

by doing something nice, such as picking a

bouquet of flowers. When we become adults, the

enemy can still tempt us to try and bribe God with

our adult versions of bouquets from the garden.

Jesus' life was the final act of sacrifice out of God's

divine love for us. Therefore, our own elaborate

atonements are not necessary to please God; He

lovingly asks that we be obedient. Our sacrifice

to the Lord can be out of our love for Him, and not

as a substitute for obedience.

P r a y e r :

Even when I fail, Lord, You are still full of grace and
mercy and love. I can be assured that if I disobey, You will
be gracious and forgiving toward me. The wonderful love
You offer makes me want to obey all the more!

If you obey my commands, you will remain in my love,
just as I have obeyed my Father's commands
and remain in his love.

JOHN 15:10

What does the Lord require of you?
To act justly and to love mercy
and to walk humbly with your God.
MICAH 6:8

*S*o often we tend to look down on positions

of service, setting our sights instead on higher

positions that appear to bring privilege, authority,

and respect. But Jesus Himself chose to be a

servant, and the greatest privilege we can have

is following His example. To lay down our rights,

our ambitions, and our lives in obedience to the

Father is actually the highest calling we can

receive. It is also the greatest offering

of thanksgiving we can give.

P r a y e r :
I am learning, Father, that You do not call me to take
giant leaps for humanity in Your name. You ask only that I
be obedient to Your will and Word. Please guide me today
in all my steps, big or small.

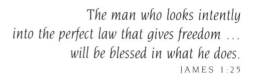

The man who looks intently
into the perfect law that gives freedom ...
will be blessed in what he does.
JAMES 1:25

God ... reconciled us to himself through Christ and gave us the ministry of reconciliation.

2 CORINTHIANS 5:18

*J*esus' life is the perfect example for teaching us about loving confrontation. Never did Christ approach a person about someone else's offense; instead, He went straight to the source and presented God's truth. Likewise, the person who has offended us will be most open if we approach him or her in a spirit of love and humility. The result will be greater unity in the body ... and we will have gained a brother or sister in Christ.

P r a y e r :
Confronting another in love is such a difficult principle to follow, Father. But when I look to Jesus, my example of loving confrontation, I receive the peace and the ability to do what You ask of me. Thank You for Your provision!

If your brother sins against you,
go and show him his fault,
just between the two of you.
If he listens to you,
you have won your brother over.

MATTHEW 18:15

He holds victory in store
for the upright,
he is a shield to those
whose walk is blameless.

PROVERBS 2:7

*A*lthough the world tends to judge us by the

perceived importance of our jobs, God rewards us

based on our faithfulness in the context of each

task, big or small. We can purpose in our hearts

that we will glorify God in our work, whatever

we do. God will allow our efforts to bring glory

to His Kingdom and joy to our lives.

P r a y e r :
Father, remind me that my source of joy
is not found in status or position, in circumstances
or in achievements. Joy is discovered only when
I look to You, the giver of joy, to guide my life.

Direct my footsteps according to your word …
that I may obey your precepts.
PSALM 119:133, 134

If we walk in the light, as he is in the light,
we have fellowship with one another.
1 JOHN 1:7

*A*s Christians and therefore representatives

of the Kingdom, we are walking test cases

for Christ's principles. If our actions are negative,

then the results toward others will be negative—

and that should be very sobering. But when our

actions are positive and lived out in obedience

to Christ, the consequences toward others are

positive and sometimes glorious—and that

should be very encouraging and motivating.

P r a y e r :
Lord, I am both honored and humbled that You want
to use my life to share Your love with the world. I am
open. May Your love begin, and may You be glorified.

Live a life worthy of the calling you have received.
EPHESIANS 4:1

Twila Paris' Booking:

William Morris Agency
2100 West End Avenue, Suite 1000
Nashville, TN 37203

Twila Paris' Publicity:

Atkins-Muse & Associates, Inc.
1808 West End Avenue
Eleventh Floor, Suite 1119
Nashville, TN 37203

Twila Paris' Management:

Proper Management
P.O. Box 150888
Nashville, TN 37215

You can write to Twila Paris at:

Twila Paris Productions
P.O. Box 20
Elm Springs, AR 72728

Look for these other fine products in the
Celebrate the Gift of Jesus Every Day™ Collection
from Warner Press, featuring *Twila Paris*,
at your local Christian Bookstore:

GREETING CARDS
(*featuring Twila Paris' song lyrics*)

BOOKMARKS
(*featuring Twila Paris' song lyrics*)

CASSETTE TAPE
(*featuring music by Twila Paris & Friends*)

ADDRESS BOOK

FRAMED, MATTED PRINT
(*featuring* Celebrate the Gift *song lyrics*)

DAILY TREASURE®
(*featuring Twila Paris' song lyrics and devotionals*)

PROMISE BOX

DESIGNER INK PEN

SCENTED CANDLE

NOTE CARDS

THANK YOU NOTES

STATIONERY

MUGS

GIFT BAGS/TISSUE PAPER